LANDSCAPING THE HAMPTONS

A GUIDE AND SOURCE BOOK

May 5 1994

To Jim Daly

In appreciation for a job
well done at the Business Alliance
as our director.

David Heller

Stonyhill Nursery, Amagansett, New York.

LANDSCAPING
THE
HAMPTONS

BY
DAVID SEELER

ILLUSTRATED BY
RALPH CARPENTIER AND TERESA PASCUAL

A GUIDE AND SOURCE BOOK
INCLUDING PLANT CHARTS

Sagapress, Inc.
Sagaponack, New York

For my mother Margaret Seeler
whose encouragement made my life in horticulture possible;
and my wife Ngaere
whose encouragement made this book possible.

Design and composition by Carol Odlum
Tigard, Oregon

Published by Sagapress, Inc.
Sagaponack, New York 11962

ISBN 0-89831-037-7

Jacket water color by Ralph Carpentier

Printed in Hong Kong

CONTENTS

Where to Begin

I PLANTED MY FIRST TREES ON LONG ISLAND when I was eight years old. It was 1949, and I had ordered fifty spruce trees from a nurseryman's mail order catalog. They arrived in a parcel the size of a shoe box, and I lined them out like carrots in my mother's vegetable garden. Two of them are still with me, giant trees spreading their graceful branches in my garden behind The Bayberry in Amagansett and reminding me of how I began in the nursery business.

With the exception of a few years away to study, I've been planting and designing gardens on Long Island ever since. And if there is one thing I have learned about this profession, it is the truth of the old saying that the more you know, the more there is to know. People tell me all the time how overwhelmed they are by the choices available to them when they begin to plan a garden or to landscape a new home. This little book may not answer all your questions, but it does describe the elements you need to consider before you begin landscaping, so that you will know what questions to ask.

Conditions on the east end of Long Island vary widely, so first you should understand the possibilities and constraints of your location. The next step is to focus on design, and to become familiar with the various levels of planning and budgets you can expect when you hire a professional designer. Finally, you need to know what to look for when buying plants, the correct way to plant them, and how to maintain them in good health.

Included are lists of plants that can be counted on to thrive in different locations: plants to feed birds or attract butterflies; shrubs and flowers for fragrance, for shade and for special situations.

The more you know, the easier it is to achieve your ideal garden. Whether you are just getting started with landscaping, or have a garden and want to improve it, here are some basic principles to build on, ideas to help you conceive your garden, and questions you should ask that will help you know *where to begin.*

1

LOOKING AT YOUR LOCATION

THE DEPARTMENT OF AGRICULTURE classifies Long Island as Plant Hardiness Zone 7, meaning that if plants are to grow here they must be able to survive temperatures as low as 0–10 °F. This generalization does not take into account elements such as wind chill in the winter and high humidity in the summer, and it is important to remember that within each zone there are considerable climatic variations. Many plants that have flourished for years in Sag Harbor wouldn't last one winter in Bridgehampton or Amagansett. The Long Island landscape falls into four distinctly different environments—seashore, farmland, woodland and wetland—and what follows is a summary of the unique problems and opportunities for landscaping that each of them presents.

Seashore

If your house sits on ocean dunes, plants that will provide shelter and privacy, yet survive in wind and salt conditions, are limited. When landscaping in sand, remember that it needs improving with peatmoss and compost before anything is planted.

© CARPENTIER

First and foremost, if it's not already there, you should introduce beach grass to anchor your landscape. This involves planting hundreds or thousands of tiny grass "plugs," and the work may be better left to a professional. If you decide to do it yourself, the plants should be spaced at one plug per square foot.

The three coastal zones have distinct characteristics and need to be considered separately.

Zone I: Very few plants will tolerate conditions from the high tide line to the top of the dune. Besides beach grass, good choices are beach wormwood, beach pea and seaside goldenrod.

Zone II: Past the lip of the dune, below the salt wind, the world changes. All native varieties thrive here and will be contoured by nature when they grow above the dune line. Juniper 'Torulosa' is one of my favorites. Not only is it good for screening, but this sturdy tree will grow at the highest level of the dune, and its branches will twist and bend into dramatic shapes from the force of the wind. Eastern red cedar, other juniper varieties and American holly (which adds a welcome touch of color to the winter landscape with its red berries) are good screening plants. Colorado blue spruce is a popular choice, although it doesn't look quite as natural in this setting. Pitch pine is native to the dunes, though it's a slow grower and tough to establish unless container-grown.

Zone III: This zone begins at a point where plants become protected by other vegetation, structures, or distance from the ocean—as a general rule at the "second dune" (where land contours begin to rise dramatically from the seascape). As long as they are protected, less tolerant varieties can be established here.

For a more complete list of recommended plants, see "Seashore Plants by Zone."

Farmland

If your house is on farmland, the chances are that you will start landscaping from scratch and your main considerations will be shelter, views, shade and privacy.

The best shelter is created by planting barriers of evergreens which insulate your house and gardens from the damaging winter winds out of the north. Shrubs and trees also provide windbreaks that allow you to plant less hardy varieties of plants in your garden. In addition to shelter, evergreens can be used to frame and accentuate views and put color into the bleak winter landscape.

Careful placement of your trees will enhance and focus the views, or screen out unsightly elements. Your views can literally be "stage-managed" by your landscaping and your living space expanded by enclosures that create extensions to your house. Native cedars are a good choice; they are hardy enough to survive heavy windstorms, and the seedling varieties vary greatly in shape and color, bringing welcome diversity to the landscape.

Shade plays an important part in making your garden inviting, particularly when you live in an open space. Decide where you need shade and, if it is close to the house, select specimen trees that are wind tolerant. Beware of trees such as willows that have

soft wood and are easily broken or upended by storms. Trees most often recommended are: Japanese pagoda, European beech and shade-master locust. Swamp maples are a good choice, but are best planted at a distance from the house because their heavy leaves tend to clog up gutters.

For privacy, consider an enclosed garden, which has the added advantage of allowing you to be more adventurous in your selection of trees and shrubs. Virtually any plant will grow in rich farm soil as long as the wind is controlled and the plant has proper drainage. For hedgerows, avoid straight lines and use native plants such as shadblow and winterberry, which look natural in the landscape. Different varieties of juniper will thrive, so be sure to consider their height when fully grown. Compact junipers, which don't grow more than three feet high, are a good choice for foundation plantings, while 'Hetzii' junipers are a better choice for screening because of their growth potential.

Woodland

In our native woodlands, trees and underbrush grow densely and compete with one another for space. This means that none of them thrive, so you will need to cull trees selectively to allow more light in and increase the air flow.

Where no thinning has ever been done, a rule of thumb is to cut down every other tree. This is a scary thought, so contact a nursery for advice before wielding your ax! Leave the stumps in the ground; they will rot away over time. And don't limit your

clearing to the vegetation beside the house—you will enjoy the views and walkways created by opening up your landscape.

It is important to know your tree canopy, as well as the shade tolerance of any trees and shrubs planted under it. Oak trees leaf out over a month later than other deciduous trees, so you can underplant with shade-tolerant evergreens such as white pines, hemlocks and Parsons junipers, and flowering shrubs such as hybrid rhododendrons, hollies, azaleas and mountain laurel.

Before you build your house or any other structures, it's a good idea to get advice from a nursery on how to site the house around large, healthy trees and take advantage of the screening and light that already exist. Where the trees have been cleared, install a few large evergreens for interest and warmth, and perhaps for privacy. A lawn adds color and an inviting space to the site, although wonderful natural landscapes can be developed without one.

If low maintenance is a goal, don't rake leaves from under the trees each fall; let them stay there as mulch. Allow native ground covers, such as huckleberry or sheep laurel, to spread. Adjust your idea of what a garden is, and think in terms of creating a woodland environment.

For a more complete list of recommended trees and shrubs, see "Plants for Woodlands or Partial Shade."

Wetland

Beware! You are in an area that is strictly controlled by local and state environmental agencies. And your neighbors are sure to contact the environmental authorities if you don't play by the rules. Most communities do not allow you to touch anything that is growing within 100 to 125 feet of the water's edge without receiving prior written approval. Your nursery will be familiar with the requirements of the town's building department, and will guide you to the authority that issues permits.

The reason for regulations is the ecological value of a wetland. Wildlife thrives in ponds, streams, swamps and bogs, so your concern should be with protecting what is already there and, wherever possible, enhancing it with paths and water views. Your

site will change dramatically as the months progress, from lowland flooding in spring to fall drought, so you should familiarize yourself with these seasonal patterns before you plant. Be sure you choose plants that can tolerate wet feet, such as swamp azalea, shadblow or white oak.

For a complete list of recommended trees, shrubs and plants, see "Plants For Wet or Very Wet Conditions."

PRINCIPLES OF DESIGN

A LANDSCAPE SHOULD BE PLANNED in much the same way as a house is planned— as a series of rooms or spaces whose sizes and shapes, and their relationship to each other, are determined by the way they are to be used. The way in which indoor and outdoor living spaces connect, both visually and physically, is the key to the success of a design.

The closer the spaces are to the house, the more they should reflect its style and architecture. These outdoor "rooms" can be achieved with the use of terraces, trellises and different grade levels. The reverse is true of the outer limits of the garden, which should visually blend into the surrounding property. This is achieved by using native plants at the outer limits of the garden, or selecting plants whose form and texture blend with the surrounding landscape. These plantings should be carefully positioned to screen less attractive features and enhance focal points, to accentuate the views and expand to the maximum the illusion of your property's dimensions.

These principles apply regardless of the size of your garden. In fact, as with designing a house, the smaller the site, the greater is the challenge to blend function with aesthetics, while still retaining the important elements of mystery and surprise.

In designing a landscape, you need to consider carefully your way of life and how you wish to use your garden. A good design takes into account every detail of the property, such as the land forms, trees and vegetation, the structure of the soil, the angle of the sun, views, and zoning requirements. Then it fits the requirements of function, form and vision onto the land. Good design should be sensitive to the natural environment, to your esthetic taste and the way you will use your garden, and, equally important, to your budget.

Once a design is established, the budget can be adjusted by substituting materials proposed for the hardscape, or changing sizes and varieties of trees and shrubs. There is usually great flexibility in these areas, but do not compromise on what are the *foundations* of any garden: drainage, grading, and preparation of quality soil for planting.

Once the plan is established you have reached the final phase which, if you get into the spirit of it, might keep you creatively occupied for the rest of your life! The trees, shrubs and flowers you choose and the way they are combined for color, texture, and fragrance, or to lure birds and butterflies, will bring your own style and taste to the garden. Your choices may cover the spectrum, from romantic English gardens overflowing with flowers to the wildflower meadows of the prairies or the stark simplicity of space and carefully placed objects that conjure up the tranquility of the Orient or, perhaps best of all, that special memory of a garden from your childhood.

COMMISSIONING A
DESIGN PROFESSIONAL

THE MOST SUCCESSFUL AND BEST-LOVED GARDENS are always the most personal. So, look for a designer who has the talent and experience to realize *your* vision. Interview designers and ask about their credentials, including years of experience and certified degrees in horticulture and landscape architecture. Look at examples of their work, and be sure they are knowledgeable about the plants that thrive here, and are familiar with the peculiarities of this region's ecology. Gardens develop slowly, so it helps to be compatible with the people with whom you choose to work. They should be around for the long haul, to give you advice on changes and additions as the garden develops.

Your options on selecting design services and fees cover a wide spectrum, from free advice on where to plant a tree or solve a technical problem, to a comprehensive study and plan prepared by a landscape architect. The following outlines what you can expect from each of the three general levels of design service.

Sketch.

THE SKETCH is a simple drawing that can solve a design or technical problem in a specific area of your property, such as a front entrance, terrace or courtyard. A design and cost estimate for this type of study can usually be done quickly by a nursery, at no charge. If a sketch requires detailed measurements, there may be a small fee.

14

DESIGN BY A NURSERY or LANDSCAPE DESIGNER is a scale drawing of your property indicating all structures, paving, driveway, existing plantings and all proposed site development. It should be accompanied by a detailed plant list specifying the size and price of all items on the plan, as well as materials and price estimates for the other hardscape elements that are included, such as terracing, trellises, fences and walls. At a good nursery, members of the staff generally have

Design by a nursery or landscape designer.

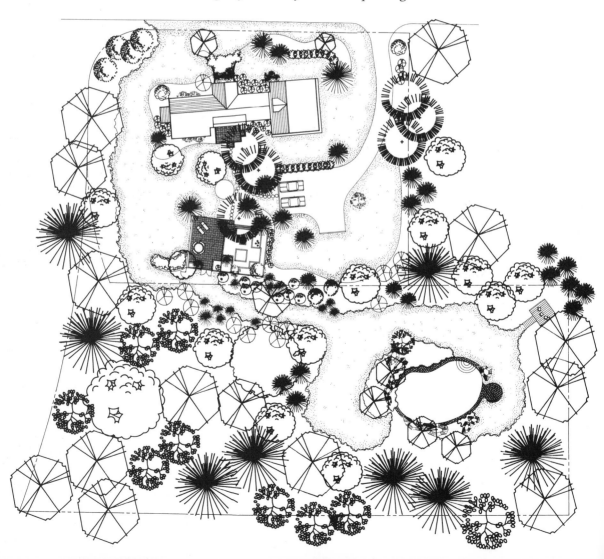

degrees in landscape architecture and horticulture and several years of field experience. They should be able to provide you with a range of design options, from detailed plans of perennial borders, cutting flower, vegetable and herb gardens, to full site development.

The design office should be computerized, and have the capability of using a computer aided design (CAD) system. This technology enables the designer to communicate electronically with CAD systems used by architects and surveyors, to merge architectural drawings with site plans and topographical maps. Thus, landscape and site plans can be developed without the extra costs normally incurred by duplication of baseline work.

Rendering of pool area from plan opposite.

Once the basic information is entered into the computer, the ability to offer landscape design options is fast and inexpensive. If you have difficulty visualizing a plan, a three-dimensional image of your site can be developed that includes all the existing or proposed buildings, amenities and plantings. Views can be projected from any places you choose. These images can be made into a slide show, which takes you on a tour of the finished project before you have even broken ground! The program factors in the growth of plants, showing you how your property will look five, ten or twenty years from now. It also calculates the exact quantity of materials such as bricks, slate or soil needed for terraces, paths or grading. Best of all, it allows you to make changes quickly, easily and inexpensively.

Fees vary depending upon the amount of development necessary. A detailed plan of perennial borders or flower and vegetable gardens may range from $150 to $350. A computerized design of the complete landscape may begin at $750 for plan view drawings and go up to several thousand dollars for a three-dimensional model. Ask for an itemized design budget in advance, and a tour of the studio and gardens to look at examples of the designer's work.

LANDSCAPE DESIGN BY A LICENSED LANDSCAPE ARCHITECT provides more comprehensive site planning, and normally includes proposals illustrating several designs. The landscape architect works closely with a surveyor and with site construction trades, and is fully responsible for and insured against any problems that occur as a result of the implementation of the drawing specifications. In New York State, a landscape architect is required to have a degree in landscape architecture and to be certified and licensed.

Landscape master plan.

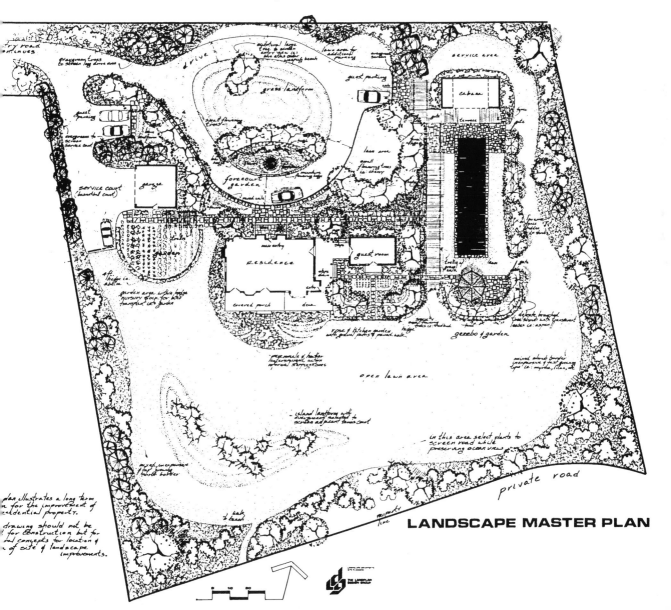

LANDSCAPE MASTER PLAN

18

Drawings and documents provided by a landscape architect include complex design; grading studies for surface and subsurface drainage and erosion control; submissions for building and other necessary permits; a master plan for landscaping, and detailed designs and technical drawings for enhancements such as pools, walls and fencing. In addition to all the above, the service typically includes illustrations, irrigation specifications, and detailed planting plans.

Costs range from $2,500 to $6,000 for studies, master plan drawings and reports. In addition, there is apt to be a fee of 10 to 20 percent of the total site development cost for managing all aspects of the project.

Grading plan.

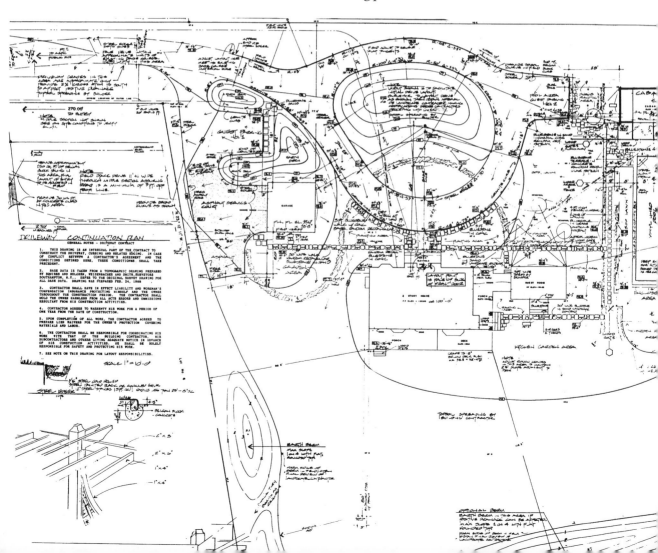

Trellis plan and details.

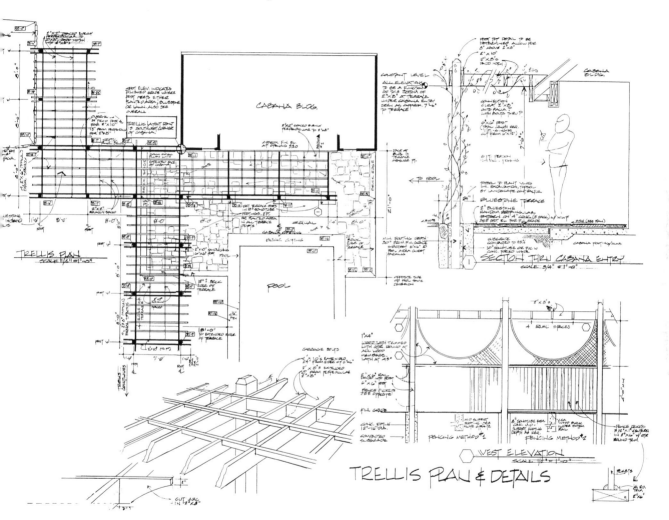

TRELLIS PLAN & DETAILS

Notes

BUDGETS AND GUARANTEES

G ENERALLY, YOUR LANDSCAPING BUDGET should be 10 to 15 percent of the cost of your new home. Of course, this figure will vary. Houses in open fields will approach the high end, while those in wooded lots will need less landscaping.

Your budget should include all site work, driveways, terraces and plantings. The plan should provide you with a total figure, which can be broken down into segments to enable you to work at a comfortable pace. It is important to understand that the budget can be increased or decreased without affecting the esthetics and integrity of the plan. This is achieved by changing the materials specified, and planting smaller (or larger) trees and shrubs. Once a contract amount is fixed, do not make changes without receiving a written estimate.

Most nurseries offer a one-year guarantee on trees and shrubs that they have planted, and a two-year guarantee on large trees that take longer to establish. Smaller plants are usually replaced immediately, even before the end of a growing season. Check the contract to see if the payment terms affect the guarantee. Standard terms state that the customer forfeits the guarantee if the invoice is not paid within 30 days. A deposit of ⅓ to ½ of the contracted sum is usually required. These terms can be adjusted and should be discussed and agreed to in advance.

Unless alternative arrangements are made, it is the customer's responsibility to ensure that proper watering and care are provided—a good reason to consider an automatic sprinkler system.

Contractors must be licensed by the town, and any complaints against them are reviewed by local authorities.

NOTES

DOING IT YOURSELF
AT THE NURSERY

THE MOST IMPORTANT THING TO REMEMBER when you are buying plants is that appearances count! The care and attention plants have received from the growers, and in the nursery, will make the difference between whether they flourish or fail in your garden. So, look for a nursery that is well cared for itself, and you will find healthy plants.

If you are overwhelmed by the choices, a good way to begin to identify what you like, and what you dislike, is to look at plants growing in your neighborhood. Take note of your favorite trees and shrubs in every season and use a dictionary of plants to identify them, or bring photographs with you to the nursery. This legwork ensures that plants you choose will thrive in your location. Also, you will know the size and shape of the plants at maturity, which is often hard to imagine when you see them in the nursery marshalled in rows, like soldiers.

Growers deliver plants to nurseries at intervals, when they are in bloom or at the best time for digging and transplanting them. So visit the nursery as often as possible and choose trees and shrubs that "perform" at different times throughout the season. If prices on large trees and shrubs are more than you want to spend, ask about smaller sizes of these same plants. If you are willing to start small and be patient, your budget will go much further.

Don't overplant! Be sure you check the size of the plants at their maturity, and GIVE THEM THE ROOM THEY NEED to grow. This will make the difference between whether your landscape looks better each year—or not.

Containers

Smaller plants are grown and sold in plastic containers and this, if the plants are properly cared for, guarantees the least amount of stress in transplanting.

If possible, avoid buying plants from southern growers. These plants will be larger and fuller than their locally grown counterparts, but they will suffer winterkill and may take years to adapt to our more extreme climate.

CONTAINER

Ball and Burlap

Larger shrubs and trees, that are dug by hand, have their roots wrapped in burlap and laced with twine. The American Association of Nurserymen standard for computing the proper size of the root-ball for a tree is the diameter of the trunk multiplied by 9. Avoid a "short ball," since the tree will not have an adequate root system. Also avoid misshapen root balls, which indicate a lack of fibrous roots (the fine capillary roots that the tree needs to absorb water).

Check the burlap bag. If roots are exposed, and the bag is disintegrating, the tree may have been out of the ground for some time. All trees are stressed by being moved, but if left above ground through the winter, the damage is compounded by freezing and thawing. For this reason, BEWARE OF SPRING SALES!

A tree that is out of the ground is out of its element, so it won't look its best. But there are some conclusions you can draw from its appearance:

◆ Are there leaves on all the branches? If not, some boughs may be dead.
◆ Do the leaves look healthy? Or are they curled up (indicating lack of water)?

BALLED AND BURLAPPED (B&B)

◆ Are there any gashes on the trunk? A tree feeds itself through the cambium, which is immediately under the bark, so a large cut can threaten its health.

◆ While evergreens do lose needles, if their branches are bare there should be new growth at the tips.

Growth Habits and Longevity. The growth habits of trees differ widely. Varieties that grow the fastest have the softest (least dense) wood, and so their life span is the shortest. They are more likely to be damaged or destroyed by storms. Examples of these soft wooded trees are maples, willows, Bradford pears and Russian olives.

The slow growers, such as beech, cryptomeria and dogwood, have denser wood and are more likely to survive coastal storms and last for generations. When you drive through the estate sections of the Hamptons, you will see that the graceful old specimen trees that frame the houses are every bit as grand and beautiful as the mansions themselves. But, unlike the houses, they are irreplaceable.

So, you can choose whether you want to plant fast-growing trees for a more immediate effect, or slow growers as a legacy for your children and future generations. If, like most people, you want a combination of both, position the trees that will last the longest where they are most important in your landscape.

Trees as Sculpture. Dwarf conifers fall into the slow-growth category and are especially well suited to small gardens, where they can be used as a focal point, like living sculpture. They are also a good choice for a hedge that has to be both dense and contained, but doesn't have to be maintained by regular clipping and pruning. Their wide range of color and unique shapes adds drama to the winter landscape.

Diseases

Species that have been introduced from overseas or from other parts of the country are more susceptible to blights than are native ones: Dutch elm disease, for example, has wiped out the entire population of American Elms. The Japanese black pine is the victim of a number of insects and viruses that are eliminating it from the Long Island landscape. Sycamores, birches and flowering dogwood are also being threatened locally. Seasonal spraying may improve survival odds but will not provide a cure or solve the problem. It is much better to get regular inspections than resort to blanket spraying. Problems can then be identified and dealt with individually, with a minimum use of insecticides. One of the advantages of using native plants is their resistance to disease.

Be sure to ASK QUESTIONS before buying your tree:

◆ Is it susceptible to disease?

◆ Where was it grown? Long Island or northeast trees are best, for they are already acclimatized to our salt air and temperature fluctuations.

◆ Should it be sheltered, or can it tolerate an exposed area?

◆ Does it require regular maintenance such as pruning and feeding?

Planting Instructions. The requirements for planting vary from plant to plant, and from site to site, so consult your nursery for specific planting instructions.

Always check that the top of the root ball is planted level with the grade. Trees that are planted too deep, even by a few inches, suffer from the equivalent of slow suffocation and either die within a few years or are so stressed that they attract every disease and virus. This is one of the commonest reasons for tree loss.

Sometimes trees are "re-bagged" during the season. If so, it is advisable to remove all but the original layer of burlap from the root ball before planting. If nylon twine has been used, cut it away from the trunk, as it will not decompose and may eventually choke the tree. Remove even sisal twine from around the trunk and fold the burlap back to the edge of the ball to ensure maximum flow of water to the roots.

Maintenance

Selecting your trees and shrubs is the easiest part of landscaping. The care, feeding and pruning that follows is what counts if you want them to thrive and look healthy. And remember that they need extra attention during the first two years while they are establishing themselves in their new location.

Regular watering is essential. If you have an irrigation system, you can program it to accommodate the areas of your property that contain new plants. Otherwise, you'll need to invest in a set of drip hoses and keep them in place for at least two growing seasons, until the plant is established. Check the foliage on your plants for any sign of stress. Faded leaf color or unsightly blemishes usually signal a problem, and the sooner it is identified, the easier it will be to rectify. Dead branches should be removed in the early spring or late fall, and a regular feeding program is always a good idea.

NOTES

A NOTE ABOUT NATIVE PLANTS

A native plant is one that has evolved and adapted to the temperature, altitude, rainfall and other variable conditions of any specific region of this diverse continent. These plants have reached a balance of existence with others that grow in their area and have developed a tolerance or immunity to local insects, funguses and diseases.

Esthetically, they give the landscape its unique character. Even more important, native plants provide food and habitat for native wildlife. This delicate balance is easily upset by the introduction of non-native plants that may be susceptible to local blight or in some cases introduce new diseases. Some do not flourish or even survive in their new environment, while others may thrive to the point of becoming invasive. When native flora is overtaken (in extreme cases), wildlife is deprived of food and shelter

Long Island's mild climate and rich soil have encouraged the introduction of a wide variety of trees and shrubs, but that does not mean they belong here. The hurricanes of 1985 and 1991 gave devastating visual proof of this, snapping huge maples in half and uprooting willows while adjacent 40-foot native cedars suffered only slight windburn!

In the plant charts that follow, natives are indicated by a diamond (♦). You may not choose to use them exclusively, but a dramatic while still natural effect can be achieved by mixing natives with specimen trees and shrubs of unusual varieties.

NOTES

PLANT CHARTS

SEASHORE PLANTS BY ZONE

LATIN NAME	COMMON NAME	T	S	E	P	G
Zone I						
◆ *Ammophila breviligulata*	◆ American Beach Grass					×
◆ *Artemisia stelleriana*	◆ Beach Wormwood				×	
◆ *Lathyrus japonicus*	◆ Beach Pea				×	
◆ *Solidago sempervirens*	◆ Seaside Goldenrod				×	

ZONE I

OLDENROD   WORMWOOD   BEACH PEA   AMERICAN BEACH GRASS

Latin name	Common name	T	S	E	P	G
Zone II (with no protection)						
◆ *Amelanchier canadensis*	◆ Shadblow		×			
Chrysanthemum nipponicum	Montauk Daisy				×	
Elaeagnus angustifolia	Russian Olive (some disease problems; Autumn Olive is better)		×			
Elaeagnus umbellata	Autumn Olive		×			
Juniperus chinensis 'Torulosa'	Torulosa Juniper	×		×		
Juniperus conferta	Shore Juniper		×	×		
Ligustrum ovalifolium	California Privet		×			
◆ *Myrica pensylvanica*	◆ Bayberry		×			
Pinus thunbergii	Japanese Black Pine (disease problems)	×		×		
◆ *Prunus maackii*	◆ Choke Cherry		×			
◆ *Prunus maritima*	◆ Beach Plum		×			
◆ *Rhus typhina*	◆ Sumac		×			
Rosa rugosa	Beach Rose				×	

ROSA RUGOSA

ZONE II · WITH NO PROTECTION
AMERICAN BEACH GRASS

T. Pascual 93

Latin name	Common name	T	S	E	P	G

Zone II (with some protection)
(Also includes all plants in Zone I)

Latin name	Common name	T	S	E	P	G
Acer pseudoplatanus	Sycamore Maple	×				
◆ *Clethra alnifolia*	◆ Sweet Pepperbush		×			
◆ *Comptonia peregrina*	◆ Sweet Fern				×	
Crataegus phaenopyrum	Washington Hawthorn	×				
Gleditsia triacanthos	Honey Locust	×				
Hydrangea macrophylla	French Hydrangea		×			
Hypericum calycinum	Hypericum		×			
Ilex glabra	Inkberry		×	×		
◆ *Ilex opaca*	◆ American Holly	×		×		
◆ *Ilex verticillata*	◆ Winterberry		×			
Juniperus var.	Spreading Juniper varieties		×	×		
◆ *Juniperus virginiana*	◆ Red Cedar	×		×		
Lonicera tatarica	Honeysuckle		×			
Picea pungens	Colorado Blue Spruce	×		×		

ZONE II WITH SOME PROTECTION

COLORADO BLUE SPRUCE · TORULOSA JUNIPER · FRENCH HYDRANGEA · LOCUST · JAPANESE BLACK PINE
HYPERICUM · YUCCA · BAYBERRY · AMERICAN BEACH GRASS · CLETHRA · VIBURNUM · HONEYSUCKLE

Latin name	Common name	T	S	E	P	G
Syringa vulgaris	Common Lilac		×			
Tamarix ramosissima	Tamarix		×			
Ulmus parvifolia	Chinese Elm	×				
◆ *Vaccinium corymbosum*	◆ High-bush Blueberry		×			
◆ *Viburnum dentatum*	◆ Arrow-wood Viburnum		×			
Viburnum opulus	Cranberry Bush Viburnum		×			
Viburnum prunifolium	Black Haw Viburnum		×			
Yucca filamentosa	Yucca				×	

Zone III
(Also includes all plants in Zones I and II)

		T	S	E	P	G
Abies concolor	White Fir	×		×		
Acer platanoides	Norway Maple	×				
◆ *Acer rubrum*	◆ Red Maple	×				
Berberis thunbergii	Barberry		×			
Cedrus atlantica	Atlas Cedar	×		×		
Chamaecyparis var.	False Cypress	×		×		
Cryptomeria japonica	Japanese Cedar	×		×		
Cytisus scoparius	Scotch Broom		×			
Euonymus var.	Euonymus		×	×		
Fagus sylvatica	European Beech	×				
Forsythia × *intermedia*	Forsythia		×			
Fraxinus americana	White Ash	×				
Fraxinus pennsylvanica	Green Ash	×				

Latin name	Common name	T	S	E	P	G
Grasses - ornamental var.	Ornamental grasses					×
Juniperus var.	Juniper		×	×		
Kolkwitzia amabilis	Beauty Bush		×			
Malus var.	Crabapple	×				
◆ *Nyssa sylvatica*	◆ Tupelo or Pepperidge	×				
Picea abies	Norway Spruce	×		×		
Pinus sylvestris	Scotch Pine	×		×		
Pyrus calleryana var.	Pear	×				
Sophora japonica	Japanese Pagoda Tree	×				
Spiraea var.	Spirea		×			
Syringa reticulata	Japanese Tree Lilac	×				
Tilia var.	Linden	×				

T. Pascual

ZONE III

WHITE FIR · CRABAPPLE · NORWAY SPRUCE · RED MAPLE · AMERICAN HOLLY · NORWAY MAPLE · EUROPEAN BEECH
VIBURNUM · BARBERRY · FORSYTHIA · SPIREA · BAYBERRY · SCOTCH BROOM · FALSE CYPRESS

NOTES

PLANTS FOR WET OR VERY WET CONDITIONS

Latin name	Common name	T	S	E	P
• *Acer rubrum*	• Red or Swamp Maple	×			
• *Amelanchier canadensis*	• Shadblow		×		
• *Aronia arbutifolia*	• Chokeberry		×		
Chionanthus virginicus	Fringe Tree	×			
• *Clethra alnifolia*	• Sweet Pepperbush		×		
Enkianthus campanulatus	Bellflower Tree		×		
Ilex glabra	Inkberry		×	×	
• *Ilex verticillata*	• Winterberry		×		
• *Kalmia latifolia*	• Mountain Laurel		×	×	

Acer rubrum

Latin name	Common name	T	S	E	P
Leucothoe var.	Leucothoe		×	×	
Liquidambar styraciflua	American Sweet Gum	×			
◆ *Nyssa sylvatica*	◆ Tupelo or Pepperidge	×			
Pieris japonica	Andromeda		×	×	
◆ *Quercus palustris*	◆ Pin Oak	×			
Rhododendron var.	Rhododendron		×	×	
Salix var.	Weeping Willow	×			
Spiraea var.	Spirea		×		
Taxodium distichum	Bald Cypress	×			
Thuja occidentalis	American Arborvitae	×		×	
Ulmus parvifolia	Chinese Elm	×			
◆ *Vaccinium* var.	◆ Blueberry		×		

Very Wet Conditions

Latin name	Common name	T	S	E	P
◆ *Acer negundo*	◆ Box Elder	×			
◆ *Acer rubrum*	◆ Red Maple	×			
Acer saccharinum	Silver Maple	×			
◆ *Alnus glutinosa*	◆ Smooth Alder	×			
◆ *Amelanchier canadensis*	◆ Shadblow	×			
◆ *Aronia arbutifolia*	◆ Chokeberry		×		
◆ *Baccharis halimifolia*	◆ High Tide Bush/ Groundsel Tree		×		
Betula nigra	River Birch	×			
Catalpa speciosa	Catalpa	×			

Latin name	Common name	T	S	E	P
Cephalanthus occidentalis	• Buttonbush		×		
Chionanthus virginicus	Fringe Tree	×			
• _Clethra alnifolia_	• Sweet Pepperbush		×		

Sweet Pepperbush
Clethra

Latin name	Common name	T	S	E	P
Cornus	Red Osier Dogwood		×		
Cytisus scoparius	Scotch Broom		×		
Elaeagnus umbellata	Autumn Olive			×	
Fraxinus pennsylvanica	Green Ash	×			
Gleditsia triacanthos	Honey Locust	×			
• _Hamamelis virginiana_	• Witch Hazel		×		

Witch Hazel

Latin name	Common name	T	S	E	P
Hypericum calycinum	Hypericum		×		
Ilex glabra	Inkberry			×	
Ilex opaca	American Holly	×		×	
Juniperus var.	Juniper		×	×	
◆ *Juniperus virginiana*	◆ Red Cedar	×		×	
◆ *Lindera benzoin*	◆ Spice Bush		×		
Liquidambar styraciflua	American Sweetgum	×			
Magnolia virginiana	Sweetbay Magnolia	×			
◆ *Myrica pensylvanica*	◆ Bayberry		×		
◆ *Nyssa sylvatica*	◆ Tupelo or Pepperidge	×			
◆ *Pinus rigida*	◆ Pitch Pine	×		×	
◆ *Prunus maritima*	◆ Beach Plum		×		
◆ *Quercus alba*	◆ White Oak	×			
◆ *Quercus palustris*	◆ Pin Oak	×			
Quercus phellos	Willow Oak	×			
◆ *Rhododendron viscosum*	◆ Swamp Honeysuckle		×		
◆ *Rhus aromatica*	◆ Fragrant Sumac		×		
Rhus typhina	Sumac		×		
◆ *Rosa palustris*	◆ Swamp Rose				×
Rosa rugosa	Rugosa Rose				×
Salix var.	Weeping Willow	×			

Latin name	Common name	T	S	E	P
♦ *Sambucus canadensis*	♦ Elder		×		
Sophora japonica	Japanese Pagoda Tree	×			
Tamarix africana	Tamarisk		×		
Taxodium distichum	Bald Cypress	×			
Tsuga canadensis	Canadian Hemlock	×		×	
Ulmus parvifolia	Chinese Elm	×			
♦ *Vaccinium corymbosum*	♦ Blueberry		×		
♦ *Viburnum dentatum*	♦ Arrow-wood Viburnum		×		
Viburnum var.	Viburnum varieties		×		

Viburnum dentatum
Arrowwood

Viburnum trilobum
Highbush Cranberry

Viburnum acerifolium
Maple leaved Viburnum

Viburnum Carlesii
Korean Spice

♦ *Yucca filamentosa*	♦ Yucca				×

Juniper

Yucca

Juniper

Locust

PLANTS FOR VERY DRY OR SANDY LOCATIONS

Latin name	Common name	T	S	E	P
Acer campestre	Hedge Maple	×			
Catalpa speciosa	Catalpa	×			
Cytisus scoparius	Scotch Broom		×		
Fraxinus var.	Ash	×			
Gleditsia var.	Locust	×			
Hypericum calycinum	Hypericum		×		
Juniperus var.	Juniper		×	×	
◆ *Myrica pensylvanica*	◆ Bayberry		×		
◆ *Prunus maritima*	◆ Beach Plum		×		
◆ *Rhus typhina*	◆ Sumac		×		
Sophora japonica	Japanese Pagoda Tree	×			
Tamarix africana	Tamarisk		×		
Ulmus parvifolia	Chinese Elm	×			
Yucca filamentosa	Yucca				×

NOTES

PLANTS FOR WOODLANDS OR PARTIAL SHADE

KEY
T = Tree
S = Shrub
E = Evergreen

Latin name	Common name	T	S	E
◆ *Amelanchier canadensis*	◆ Shadblow	×		
Aralia spinosa	Five-leaf Aralia		×	
◆ *Aronia arbutifolia*	◆ Chokeberry		×	
Berberis thunbergii	Barberry		×	
◆ *Calycanthus floridus*	◆ Sweet Shrub		×	
Chionanthus virginicus	Fringe Tree	×		
◆ *Cornus florida*	◆ Flowering Dogwood	×		

Dogwood

Cornus kousa	Japanese Dogwood	×		
Cornus kousa var. *chinensis*	Chinese Dogwood	×		

Latin name	Common name	T	S	E
Euonymous var.	Euonymus varieties		×	×
• *Hamamelis virginiana*	• Witch Hazel		×	
Hydrangea var.	Hydrangea		×	
Ilex var.	Holly		×	×
• *Kalmia latifolia*	• Mountain Laurel		×	×

Mountain Laurel

| *Kolkwitzia amabilis* | Beauty Bush | | × | |
| *Ligustrum* var. | Privet varieties | | × | |

Latin name	Common name	T	S	E
Magnolia var.	Magnolia	×		

Magnolia

Latin name	Common name	T	S	E
Oxydendrum arboreum	Sourwood	×		
Photinia villosa	Photinia		×	
Phyllostachys	Bamboo		×	
Pieris japonica	Andromeda		×	×
◆ *Pinus strobus*	◆ White Pine	×		×
Pyracantha var.	Pyracantha varieties		×	×
Rhododendron var.	Rhododendron		×	×
Symphoricarpos orbiculatus	Coralberry		×	
Taxus var.	Yew		×	×
Tsuga canadensis	Canadian Hemlock	×		×
Viburnum var.	Viburnum		×	

NOTES

Key
T = Tree
S = Shrub
E = Evergreen

Latin name	Common name	Blooms				
		Spring	May	June	Fall	Fragrance
Abelia × grandiflora	Abelia (S)				×	×
Buddleia davidii	Butterfly Bush (S)			×	×	×
Calycanthus floridus	Sweet Shrub (S)					×
Caryopteris × clandonensis	Blue Mist (S)				×	
Chaenomeles speciosa	Quince (S)	×				
Cornus kousa	Japanese Dogwood (T)					
Cornus kousa var. *chinensis*	Chinese Dogwood (T)	×				

Sweet Shrub

Daphne

Blue Mist

Hypericum

Butterfly Bush

Latin name	Common name	Blooms				
		Spring	May	June	Fall	Fragrance
Cytisus scoparius	Scotch Broom (S)					×
Daphne cneorum	Daphne (S)					×
Deutzia gracilis	Deutzia (S)	×				×
Elaeagnus var.	Olives (ES or S)					×
Fothergilla gardenii	Fothergilla (S)	×				
Hypericum calycinum	Hypericum (S)				×	
Kerria japonica	Kerria (S)	×				
Kolkwitzia amabilis	Beauty Bush (S)		×			
Lonicera tatarica	Bush Honeysuckle (S)	×	×			
Magnolia var.	Magnolia (T)	×	×	×		
Malus var.	Crabapple (T)	×				×
• *Philadelphus coronarius*	• Mock Orange (S)			×		×
Prunus glandulosa	Flowering Almond (S)					×
Prunus var.	Cherry (T)	×				×
Rhododendron var.	Rhododendron (ES)	×	×	×		
Rosa var.	Rose varieties (S)			×		×
Spiraea var.	Spirea (S)	×				
Syringa vulgaris	Common Lilac (S)					×
Tamarix africana	Tamarisk (S)				×	
Viburnum var.	Viburnum (S)	×	×			×
Vitex negunda	Vitex (S)				×	

BERRY-BEARING SHRUBS AND TREES

Key
T = Tree
S = Shrub
E = Evergreen
P = Perennial

Latin name	Common name	T	S	E	P
Red Berries					
Aronia arbutifolia	Chokeberry		×		
Berberis thunbergii	Barberry		×		
Cornus kousa	Japanese Dogwood	×			
Cornus kousa var. *chinensis*	Chinese Dogwood	×			
Cotoneaster var.	Cotoneaster		×		
Crataegus var.	Hawthorn	×			
Euonymous var.	Euonymus		×	×	
Ilex opaca	American Holly	×		×	
Ilex verticillata	Winterberry		×		
Lindera benzoin	Spice Bush		×		
Lonicera tatarica	Honeysuckle Bush		×		
Magnolia var.	Magnolia		×		
Malus var.	Crabapple		×		

Latin name	Common name	T	S	E	P
Pyracantha var.	Pyracantha		×	×	
Rhus typhina	Sumac		×		
Rosa var.	Rose varieties				×
Sorbus aucuparia	Mountain Ash	×			
Symphoricarpos orbiculatus	Coralberry		×		
Viburnum var.	Viburnum		×		

Pyracantha

Sumac

Latin name	Common name	T	S	E	P
Black Berries					
Amelanchier canadensis	Shadblow	×			
Ilex crenata	Japanese Holly		×	×	
Ilex glabra	Inkberry		×	×	
Ligustrum var.	Privet		×		
Viburnum var.	Viburnum		×		
White Berries					
Cornus var.	Dogwood varieties		×		
Myrica pensylvanica	Bayberry		×		
Pachysandra terminalis	Pachysandra			×	×
Symphoricarpos orbiculatus alba	Coralberry		×		
Deep Blue Berries					
Berberis julianae	Barberry (julianae)			×	
Viburnum var.	Viburnum		×		

Bayberry

NOTES

FOR THE BIRDS

KEY
T = Tree
S = Shrub
E = Evergreen

LATIN NAME	COMMON NAME	T	S	E
◆ *Amelanchier canadensis*	◆ Shadblow	✕	✕	
◆ *Aronia arbutifolia*	◆ Chokeberry		✕	
Berberis thunbergii	Barberry			✕
Betula var.	Birch	✕		
◆ *Cornus florida*	◆ Flowering Dogwood	✕		
Cornus mas	Cornelian Cherry Dogwood	✕		
Cornus stolonifera	Red Osier Dogwood		✕	
Cotoneaster var.	Cotoneaster		✕	
Crataegus var.	Hawthorne	✕		
Elaeagnus angustifolia	Russian Olive		✕	
Euonymous var.	Euonymus		✕	
Fagus var.	Beech	✕		

Latin name	Common name	T	S	E
Ilex glabra	Inkberry		×	×
Ilex var.	Holly	×		×
✦ *Ilex verticillata*	✦ Winterberry		×	
✦ *Juniperus virginiana*	✦ Red Cedar	×		×
Kolkwitzia amabilis	Beauty Bush		×	
Larix decidua	European Larch	×		
✦ *Lindera benzoin*	✦ Spice Bush		×	
Lonicera tatarica	Honeysuckle		×	
Malus var.	Crabapple	×		
Morus alba	Mulberry	×		
✦ *Myrica pensylvanica*	✦ Bayberry		×	
✦ *Nyssa sylvatica*	✦ Tupelo	×		
Phellodendron amurense	Amur Cork Tree	×		
Pinus var.	Pine varieties	×		×
Prunus × cistena	Sand Cherry		×	
✦ *Prunus maritima*	✦ Beach Plum		×	
Prunus var.	Cherry	×		
Prunus var.	Plum	×		
Pyracantha var.	Firethorn		×	×
✦ *Rhus typhina*	✦ Sumac		×	
Rosa var.	Rose varieties		×	

Latin name	Common name	T	S	E
◆ *Sambucus* var.	◆ Elder	×		
◆ *Sassafras albidum*	◆ Sassafras	×		
Sorbus aucuparia	Mountain Ash	×		
Symphoricarpos albus	Snowberry		×	
Symphoricarpos orbiculatus	Coralberry		×	
Taxus var.	Yew			×
Tsuga canadensis	Canadian Hemlock	×		×
Ulmus parvifolia	Chinese Elm	×		
◆ *Vaccinium corymbosum*	◆ Blueberry		×	
Viburnum var.	Viburnum		×	

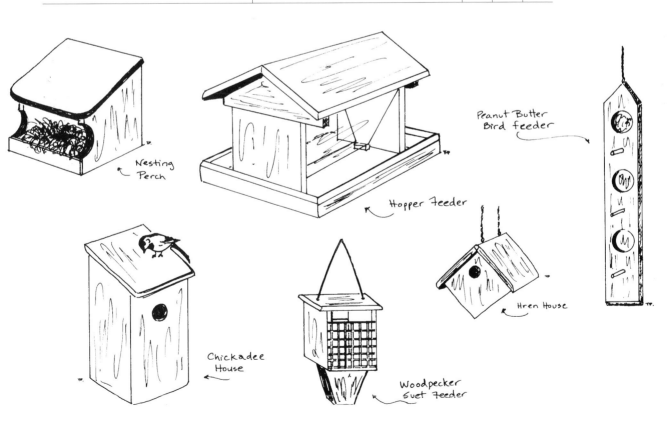

Nesting Perch

Hopper Feeder

Peanut Butter Bird feeder

Chickadee House

Woodpecker Suet Feeder

Hren House

NOTES

Rabbit-proof Shrubs

Key
T = Tree
S = Shrub
E = Evergreen

Latin name	Common name	T	S	E
◆ *Amelanchier canadensis*	◆ Shadblow	×	×	
◆ *Aronia arbutifolia*	◆ Chokeberry		×	
Aucuba japonica	Aucuba		×	×
Buddleia davidii	Butterfly Bush		×	
Chaenomeles speciosa	Quince		×	
◆ *Clethra alnifolia*	◆ Sweet Pepper Bush		×	
Cotoneaster var.	Cotoneaster		×	
Daphne cneorum	Daphne		×	
Deutzia gracilis	Deutzia		×	
◆ *Ilex verticillata*	◆ Winterberry		×	
◆ *Kalmia latifolia*	◆ Mountain Laurel		×	×
Ligustrum var.	Privet		×	
◆ *Myrica pensylvanica*	◆ Bayberry		×	
Philadelphus coronarius	Mock Orange		×	

Latin name	Common name	T	S	E
Phyllostachys	Bamboo		×	

Bamboo

Pieris japonica	Andromeda		×	×

Andromeda

Latin name	Common name	T	S	E
Prunus caroliniana	Cherry Laurel		×	×
◆ *Prunus maritima*	◆ Beach Plum		×	
Rhododendron var.	Rhododendron		×	×
◆ *Rhus typhina*	◆ Sumac		×	
◆ *Vaccinium corymbosum*	◆ Blueberry		×	

Blueberry

NOTES

Deer-resistant Shrubs

Key
T = Tree
S = Shrub
E = Evergreen
P = Perennial

Latin name	Common name	T	S	E	P
♦ *Amelanchier canadensis*	♦ Shadblow		×		
♦ *Aronia arbutifolia*	♦ Chokeberry		×		
Berberis thunbergii	Barberry		×		
Buddleia davidii	Butterfly Bush		×		
Chaenomeles speciosa	Quince		×		
♦ *Clethra alnifolia*	♦ Sweet Pepper Bush		×		
Cotinus coggygria	Smoke Bush (green only)		×		
Cytisus scoparius	Scotch Broom		×		
Daphne cneorum	Daphne		×		
Forsythia × intermedia	Forsythia		×		

Forsythia

Latin name	Common name	T	S	E	P
Hypericum calycinum	Hypericum		×		
◆ *Ilex verticillata*	◆ Winterberry		×		
Kerria japonica	Kerria		×		
Leucothoe var.	Leucothoe		×		
Ligustrum var.	Privet		×		
Magnolia var.	Magnolia		×		
◆ *Myrica*	◆ Bayberry		×		
Philadelphus coronarius	Mock Orange		×		
Phyllostachys	Bamboo		×		
Pieris japonica	Andromeda		×	×	
◆ *Prunus maritima*	◆ Beach Plum		×		
Rhododendron var.	Rhododendron		×	×	
Spiraea var.	Spirea		×		
◆ *Vaccinium corymbosum*	◆ Blueberry		×		
Viburnum var.	Viburnum		×		
Weigela floribunda	Weigela		×		
Yucca filamentosa	Yucca				×

Low-maintenance Perennials for Sun

This list contains easy-to-grow perennials. Many more varieties are available.

*Note: not to be cut back in fall

Latin name	Common name	Color	Height	Blooms
Achillea	Yarrow	Various	18–30"	June
Achillea taygeta	Yarrow	Yellow	18–24"	June
Anemone japonica	Japanese Anemone	White, pink	24–36"	Sept
Armeria maritima	Sea Thrift	Near red	6"	June/again in Aug
Aruncus sylvester	Goatsbeard	White	5'	June
Asclepia	Butterfly Weed	Orange	18–24"	June–Sept
Astilbe, assorted	Astilbe	Various	6–36"	Various
Baptisia australis	False Indigo	Blue	3–5'	May
Buddleia	Butterfly Bush	Various	4–6'	Aug
Caryopteris	Blue Mist	Blue	2–3'	July
Centaurea montana	Bachelor's Button	Blue	24"	May
Centaurea dealbata	Bachelor's Button	Pink	24"	June
Centranthus ruber	Valeriana	White, pink	18–24"	June–Sept
Ceratostigma	Plumbago	Blue	10–12"	July

Latin name	Common name	Color	Height	Blooms
Chrysanthemum pacificum	Gold and Silver Chrysanthemum	Yellow	24"	Oct
Chrysanthemum maximum	Shasta	White	8–14"	June
Coreopsis	Tickseed	Pink, yellow	12–24"	June
Cineraria	Dusty Miller	Silver leaves	12"	
Crocosmia	Crocosmia	Orange, yellow	3'	July*
Dianthus	Cheddar Pink	Pink	5–8"	May
Dicentra	Bleeding Heart	White, pink	12–30"	

Penstemon   Perovskia   Echinacea   Platycoden   Physostegia   Hemerocallis

Phlox subulata   Nepeta   Achillea   Veronica   Anemone japo

LATIN NAME	COMMON NAME	COLOR	HEIGHT	BLOOMS
Echinacea	Coneflower	White, pink, red	2–4'	July–Sept
Eupatorium coelestinum	Ageratum	White, blue	2'	July–Sept
Euphorbia	Spurge	Chartreuse	12–15"	May

beckia   Clematis   Coreopsis   Iris kaempferi   Paeonia   Sedum

cosmia   Ceratostigma   Centranthus   Caryopteris   Asclepia   Helianthemum

Latin name	Common name	Color	Height	Blooms
Gaillardia	Blanket Flower	Red, yellow	8–24"	June–Sept
Gaura	Gaura	White	3'	June–Sept
Geranium	Sanguineum	Various	1'	May
Geum	Geum (Avens)	Orange, yellow	14–24"	June
Gypsophila	Baby's Breath	Pink	18"	June
Helenium	Sneezeweed	Orange, yellow	3–4'	July–Sept
Helianthemum	Sun Rose	Various	12"	May[*]
Hemerocallis	Daylily	Various	11–40"	June–Sept
Heuchera	Coral Bell	White, coral	20"	May–July
Hibiscus	Rose Mallow	White, red, pink	3–4'	July
Hypericum	St John's Wort	Yellow	12–24"	June
Iberis	Candytuft	White	7"	May
Iris kaempferi	Japanese Iris	Various	36"	June
Iris siberica	Siberian Iris	Various	15–36"	May
Lavendula	Lavender	White, purple	12–15"	June[*]
Lythrum	Purple Loosestrife	Pink, purple	3–4'	June
Nepeta	Catmint	Blue, white	1–3'	June
Penstemon	Beard Tongue	Blue, red, pink	12–20"	June

LATIN NAME	COMMON NAME	COLOR	HEIGHT	BLOOMS
Perovskia	Russian Sage	Silver leaves	3–4'	July
Phlox subulata	Moss Phlox	White, pink, blue	4–6"	April
Physostegia	False Dragonhead	White	2'	July
Potentilla	Cinquefoil	Yellow, orange, red	3–14"	June
Rudbeckia	Black-eyed Susan	Yellow	1–5'	July
Rudbeckia triloba	Brown-eyed Susan	Yellow	2'	July
Santolina	Lavender Cotton	Yellow	6–12"	June
Scabiosa	Pincushion Flower	White, blue	15–24"	June
Sedum	Stonecrop	Various	3–24"	Various
Sidalcea	False Mallow	White, pink	3'	July
Statice latifolia	Sea Lavender	Blue	18-24"	July
Stokesia	Stokes Aster	White, blue	12–18"	July
Veronica virginica	Speedwell	White	3'	July

NOTES

Low-maintenance Perennials for Semi-shade

Latin name	Common name	Color	Height	Blooms
Acanthus	Bear's Breeches	Pink, mauve	3–4'	Aug
Ajuga	Bugle	Pink, blue	6–8'	May
Anemone japonica	Japanese Anemone	White, pink	2–3'	Sept
Alchemilla	Lady's Mantle	Chartreuse	6–18"	June
Aquilegia	Columbine	Various	6–30"	May
Aruncus	Goatsbeard	Creamy white	4–5'	June–July
Astilbe	Astilbe	White, pink, red	6–36"	July
Baptisia	False Indigo	Blue	3–5'	June–Aug
Bergenia	Bergenia	Pink, red	12–15"	April
Brunnera	Anchusa	Blue	12"	May
Campanula	Bellflower	Blue, white	6"–2'	June–July
Ceratostigma	Plumbago	Blue	10–12"	July
Chelone	Turtlehead	White, pink	3'	Aug
Chrysanthemum maximum	Shasta Daisy	White	8"–30"	May–July

Baptisia   Lythrum   Rodgersia   Heuchera Physostegia Alehemilla Hydrangea Polygonat
Dicentra Chrysanthemum maximum   Coreopsis Lupine Aruncus Digitalis Geranium sanguineu

Latin name	Common name	Color	Height	Blooms
Cimicifuga	Snakeroot	White	6'	Aug
Coreopsis	Tickseed	Yellow, pink	12–24"	June
Dicentra	Bleeding Heart	White, pink	12–30"	June
Digitalis	Foxglove	Various	4–5'	June–July
Eupatorium	Ageratum	White, blue	2'	Aug–Oct
Euphorbia	Spurge	Chartreuse	12–15"	May
Filipendula	Meadow Sweet	Pink, white	15"–4'	June–Aug
Galium	Sweet Woodruff	White	2–8"	June
Geranium sanguineum	G. 'Shepherd's Warning'	White, pink	1'	May
Geum	Geum (Avens)	Yellow, orange	14–24"	June
Hemerocallis	Daylily	Various	11–40"	June–Sept
Hosta	Plaintain Lily	White, blue	19–36"	June
Heuchera	Coral Bells	White, coral	20"	May–July
Iris kaempferi	Japanese Iris	Various	3'	June
Iris siberica	Siberian Iris	Various	15–36"	May
Lamium	Spotted Nettle	Silvery leaves	4–8"	May

Latin name	Common name	Color	Height	Blooms
Ligularia	Groundsel	Yellow	4'	June–Aug
Lupinus	Lupine	Various	30"	June
Lythrum	Purple Loosestrife	Pink, purple	3–4'	June
Physostegia	False Dragonhead	White	2'	July
Polygonatum	Solomon's Seal	White	12–15"	May
Pulmonaria	Lungwort	Pink, turns blue	8–12"	April
Rodgersia	Rodgersia	Pinkish cream	3–5'	July
Rudbeckia	Black-eyed Susan	Yellow	1–5'	July
Thalictrum	Meadow Rue	Yellow, lavender	3–6'	June
Tiarella	Foam flower	White	4–12"	May
Veronica virginica	Speedwell	White	3'	July

Perennials That Can Tolerate Full Shade

Latin name	Common name	Color	Height	Blooms
Acanthus	Bear's Breeches	Pink, purple	3–4'	Aug
Aegopodium	Goatweed	White	10–15"	May
Ajuga reptans	Bugle	Pink, blue	6–8"	May
Alchemilla	Lady's Mantle	Chartreuse	6–18"	June
Aquilegia	Columbine	Various	6–30"	May
Astilbe	Astilbe	White, pink, red	6–36"	July
Bergenia	Bergenia	Red, pink	12–15"	April
Brunnera	Anchusa	Blue	1'	May
Convallaria	Lily of the Valley	White, pink	8–10"	May
Dodecatheon meadia	Shooting Star	Blush	10"	May
Cimicifuga	Snakeroot	White	2–5'	Aug
Epimedium	Barrenwort	Various	6–12"	May
Fern	Various varieties	Green leaves	9"–6'	Some are evergreen
Galax	Galax	White	8–15"	May–June
Galium	Sweet Woodruff	White	6–8"	May
Gentian	Gentian	Blue	1'	July

Latin name	Common name	Color	Height	Blooms
Iris cristata	Crested Iris	Blue	6"	June
Houttuynia	Houttuynia	Bronze/red leaves	6–8"	July–Aug
Helleborus	Hellebore	Off white, lavender	14–16"	March
Hosta	Plaintain Lily	White, lilac	18"–5'	July
Lamium	Spotted Dead Nettle	White, pink	8"	May
Ligularia	Golden Groundsel	Orange, yellow	36–40"	July
Lilium philadelphicum	Wood Lily	Red, orange	1–3'	June
Lilium superbum	Turk's-cap	Orange	3–6'	July
Liriope	Lily Turf	White, violet	1–2'	July
Mertensia	Virginia Bluebell	Pink to blue	1–2'	May
Myosotis	Forget-me-not	Bright blue	8"	May–Aug
Phlox stolonifera	Early Phlox	White, pink, blue	8"	May
Polygonatum	Solomon's Seal	White	12–15"	May
Trillium	Wake-robin	White	10–15"	May

Houttuynia   Cimcifuga Bergenia Hemerocallis Hydrangea a. petiolaris
Astilbe   Hosta   Fern   Lamium Ligularia Epimedium Hydrangea

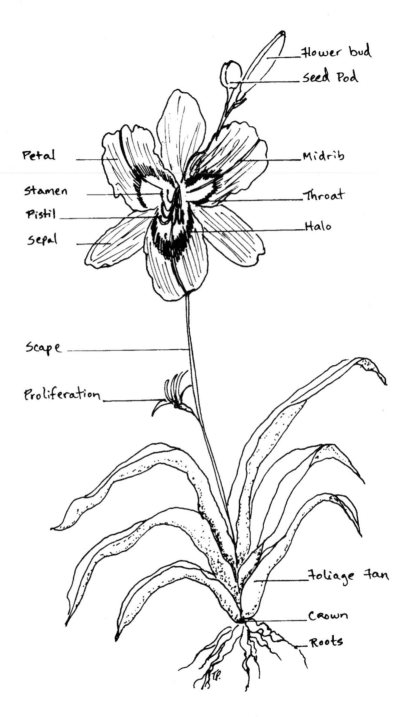

Flower bud

Seed Pod

Petal

Midrib

Stamen

Throat

Pistil

Halo

Sepal

Scape

Proliferation

Foliage Fan

Crown

Roots

Hemerocallis

Daylilies by Season and Color

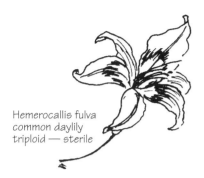

Hemerocallis fulva
common daylily
triploid — sterile

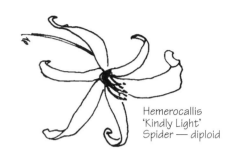

Hemerocallis
'Kindly Light'
Spider — diploid

KEY
EM = Early–Middle
M = Middle
ML = Middle–Late
L = Late

Common name	Flowering Season				Color	Height
	EM	M	ML	L		
Across the Miles	✕				Lemon yellow	32"
Admiral	✕				Red	36"
Alice in Wonderland		✕			Lemon yellow	32"
Amazon Amethyst	✕				Mauve	35"
Annie Welch	✕				Flesh pink	24"
April Dawn	✕				Peach	30"
Bicentennial	✕				Rose pink	28"
Big Wig				✕	Gold	34"
Border Giant		✕			Melon	15"
Brook Master		✕			Orchid pink	32"

Common name	Flowering Season				Color	Height
	EM	M	ML	L		
Butter Pat		×			Light yellow	20"
Christmas Carol	×				Crimson red	34"
Circus Clown			×		Pink blend	28"
Classic Simplicity	×				Light yellow	34"
Cocktail Date	×				Peach	28"
Cool Streams		×			Yellow	28"
Deep Purple	×				Dark purple	26"
Doll's House	×				Tangerine	27"
Dresden Beauty			×		Lavender	30"
Fabulous Flame		×			Pink	30"
Fifty Grand		×			Bright yellow	32"
Flaming Poppa			×		Flame red	26"
Franz Hals			×		Yellow & brick	22"
Gentle Blessing		×			Light yellow	33"
Geraldine Dean		×			Cream rose	36"
Giant Fling		×			Yellow	34"

Common name	Flowering Season				Color	Height
	EM	M	ML	L		
Golden Chance	✕				Gold	28"
Grand Ways	✕				Rose	26"
Grecian Key		✕			Lavender	32"
Hallowell	✕				Yellow	34"
Heart to Heart			✕		Red	34"
Holiday Wreath	✕				Dark red	24"
Hortensia		✕			Yellow	34"
Hot Toddy		✕			Pink	25"
Ice Carnival		✕			Ivory	28"
Intricate Art		✕			Yellow	24"
Irish Acres	✕				Yellow	30"
Jay		✕			Rose red	24"
July Gold			✕		Gold	28"
Little Love			✕		Melon	26"
Little Tyke		✕			Red	20"
Lively Set			✕		Peach	34"
Luxury Lace		✕			Lavender	32"
May Hall				✕	Orchid	30"
Moon Jet		✕			Yellow	32"
Music Man		✕			Red	28"

Common name	Flowering Season				Color	Height
	EM	M	ML	L		
My Funny Valentine	×				Rose pink	24"
Mystery Valley			×		Coral	28"
Oriental Influence		×			Lavender	34"
Painted Sculpture	×				Pink	28"
Party Partner			×		Apricot	32"
Patio			×		Pink	30"
Peach Pinwheel			×		Light pink	26"
Pink Embers	×				Salmon pink	20"
Plus	×				Red	36"
Ponchita		×			Peach	30"
Peppermint Parfait			×		Coral	30"
Prairie Butterfly		×			Pink	32"
Spring Chimes			×		Yellow	36"
Stella d'Oro	×			×	Gold	12"
Tahitian Torch			×		Pink	32"
Tailspin		×			Salmon	30"
Tina Ranae	×				Peach	36"
Touch of Mink	×				Yellow	35"
Toyland		×			Tangerine	22"

COMMON NAME	FLOWERING SEASON				COLOR	HEIGHT
	EM	M	ML	L		
Treasure Shores			×		Pink	36"
Tropic Tangerine	×				Tangerine	34"
Wild Heart			×		Red	24"
Wild Welcome			×		Apricot	34"
Wish Away				×	Melon	34"
Young Countess		×			Pink	26"

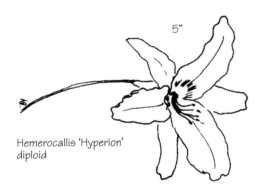

Hemerocallis 'Hyperion'
diploid

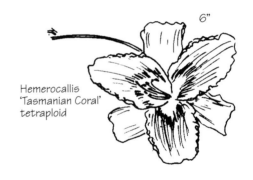

Hemerocallis
'Tasmanian Coral'
tetraploid

Hemerocallis 'King Alfred'
double — tetraploid

Hemerocallis fulva clone
double — triploid

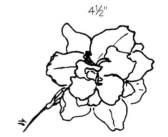

Hemerocallis 'Staci Cox'
double — diploid

NOTES

HERBS

KEY
P = Perennial
A = Annual
B = Biennial
TP = Tender Perennial
PS = Partial Sun

HERB GARDEN

COMMON NAME	USE	TYPE	HEIGHT	SUN SHADE	SOIL
Aloe	Medicinal	TP	12"	Sun	Pot
Alpine Strawberry	Culinary	P	6–10"	PS	Rich
Angelica	Medicinal, fragrance	B	3–8'	PS	Rich
Arugula	Culinary	A	12"	Sun	Good
Artemisia, Silver	Dried	A	18"	Sun	Good
Balm, Lemon	Medicinal, culinary, fragrance	P	18"	Sun/PS	Any
Basil (Sweet, Opal)	Culinary	A	3'	Sun	Rich
Basil, Dwarf	Culinary, fragrance	A	12"	Sun	Rich
Basil, Cinnamon	Tea	A	2–3'	Sun	Rich
Bee Balm (Monarda)	Tea	P	2'	PS	Good
Catnip	Cats, tea	P	2'	Sun	Any

Common name	Use	Type	Height	Sun Shade	Soil
Chamomile, Roman	Tea, fragrance	P	6–8"	Sun/PS	Rich
Chamomile, Dyer's Yellow	Dye, tea	P	2–3'	Sun	Good
Chives (Alium, Garlic)	Culinary	P	2'	Sun	Good
Clove Pinks (Dianthus)	Culinary	P	12–15"	PS	Rich
Comfrey	Medicinal	P	3–4'	PS	Rich
Coriander/Cilantro	Culinary	A	2'	Sun	Good
Curry	Culinary, fragrance	TP	18"	Sun/PS	Good
Dill	Culinary	A	18"	Sun	Good
Echinacea	Medicinal	P	2–3'	Sun	Good
Fennel	Culinary	P	3–5	Sun	Good
Feverfew	Medicinal, tea	P	2–3'	Sun/PS	Good
Hyssop	Dye, fragrance	P	2'	Sun	Any
Jasmine	Fragrance	TP	Climber	Sun	Rich
Lavender	Frag, tea	P	2'	Sun	Sandy
Lemon Verbena	Medicinal, fragrance	TP	3–4'	Sun	Container
Marjoram	Culinary, fragrance	TP	8–12"	Sun	Good
Mints, Peppermint	Tea, fragrance	P	1–3'	PS	Any

Common name	Use	Type	Height	Sun Shade	Soil
Mints, Spearmint	Tea, fragrance	P	1–3'	PS	Any
Nasturtium	Culinary, fragrance	A	8–12"	Sun	Any
Oregano (Greek)	Culinary, fragrance	P	10–12"	Sun	Sandy
Oregano (True)	Culinary, fragrance	P	12"	Sun	Sandy
Parsley (Flat/Curly)	Culinary, medicinal	B	12"	PS	Rich
Pennyroyal	Pets, fragrance	P	6–8"	PS	Good
Pyrethrum	Pets, culinary	P	30"	Sun	Good
Rosemary	Culinary, fragrance	TP	3'	Sun	Container
Rue	Culinary, dye	P	30"	Sun	Good
Sage	Culinary, fragrance	P	2–3'	Sun	Sandy/good
Sage, Tricolor	Culinary	TP	18"	Sun	Sandy/good
St John's Wort	Medicinal, dye	P	40"	Sun/PS	Rich
Safflower	Dye	A	4–5'	Sun	Good
Savory, Winter	Culinary, fragrance	P	12–18"	Sun	Sandy/good
Sweet Myrtle	Topiary	TP	12–18"	Sun	Container

Common name	Use	Type	Height	Sun Shade	Soil
Tansy (Gray)	Tea, dye, fragrance	P	5'	Sun	Good
Tarragon, French	Culinary	P	18–24"	PS	Rich
Thyme, English	Culinary, fragrance	P	10–12"	Sun	Well drained
Thyme, Lemon	Culinary, fragrance	P	8"	Sun	Well drained
Valerian	Medicinal, fragrance	P	2–5'	Sun	Good
Wormwood	Repel	P	3–4'	Sun/Shade	Any

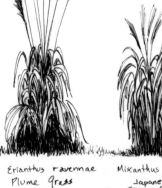

20'
19'
18'
17'
16'
15'
14'
13'
12'
11'
10'
9'
8'
7'
6'
5'
4'
3'
2'
1'
0'

Miscanthus floridulus
Giant Miscanthus

Erianthus ravennae
Plume grass

Miscanthus sinensis
Japanese
Silver grass

Calamagrostis a.
Feather Reed
grass

Spartina p.
Cord grass

Panicum
switch grass

Pennisetum a.
Fountain grass

Uniola l.
Northern
Sea Oats

Ornamental Grasses

Latin name	Common name	Height
Ground Cover in Partial or Full Shade		
Carex comans	New Zealand Hair Sedge	1–2'
C. digitata	Sedge	8"
C. morrowii 'Variegata'	Golden-variegated Japanese Sedge	1'
C. pendula	Drooping Sedge Grass	2–3'
C. plantaginea	Plantain-leaved Sedge Grass	1–2'
Luzula nivea & cultivars	Snowy Wood Rush	2'
L. sylvatica & cultivars	Greater Wood Rush	1'
Phalaris arundinacea 'Picta'	Ribbon Grass	2–3'
Ground Cover in Sun		
Briza media	Quaking Grass	2–3'
Calamagrostis × *acutiflora* 'Stricta'	Feather Reed Grass	5–7'
Deschampsia cespitosa & cultivars	Tufted Hair Grass	2'
Festuca cinerea & cultivars	Blue Sheep Fescue	8"
F. tenuifolia	Fine-leaved Fescue	8"
Helictotrichon sempervirens	Blue Oat Grass	2'
Pennisetum alopecuroides	Fountain Grass	3–4'
P. a. 'Hameln'	Dwarf Fountain Grass	1–2'
Sesleria autumnalis	Autumn Moor Grass	1'

Helictotrichon Blue Oat grass · Elymus a. Blue Lyme grass · Phalaris Ribbon grass · Pennisetum hameln Dwarf Fountain grass · Imperata c. Japanese Blood grass · Koeleria m. Blue June grass · Descampsia Hair grass · Hakonechloa Pitscale grass · Festuca a Blue Fescue · Carex m. Japanese sedge grass

6'
5'
4'
3'
2'
1'
0

Latin name	Common name	Height
For Arrangements		
Arundo donax	Giant Reed Grass	9–12'
Briza media	Quaking Oat Grass	2–3'
Chasmanthium latifolium	Wild Oats	3'
Erianthus ravennae	Ravenna Grass	9–12'
Miscanthus species & cultivars	Silver Grass	5–7'
Panicum virgatum & cultivars	Switch Grass	5–8'
Pennisetum alopecuroides	Fountain Grass	3–4'
P. incomptum	Fountain Grass	3–4'
Sesleria autumnalis	Autumn Moor Grass	1'
Sorghastrum avenaceum	Indian Grass	4–6'
Spartina pectinata	Prairie Cord Grass	4–6'
S. p. 'Aureomarginata'	Variegated Cord Grass	5–7'
Seashore		
Chasmanthium latifolium	Wild Oats	3'
Elymus glaucus	Blue Wild Rye	2-3'
Erianthus ravennae	Ravenna Grass	9–12'
Panicum virgatum & cultivars	Switch Grass	5–8'
Phalaris arundinacea 'Picta'	Ribbon Grass	3'
Phragmites australis & cultivars	Common Reed Grass	19'
Spartina pectinata & cultivars	Prairie Cord Grass	4–6'
Specimen Varieties		
Arundo donax	Giant Reed Grass	9–12'
Erianthus ravennae	Ravenna Grass	9–12'

Latin name	Common name	Height
Miscanthus floridulus	Giant Chinese Silver Grass	8–10'
M. sinensis condensatus	Purple Japanese Silver	6–8'
M. s. 'Gracillimus'	Maiden Grass	5–8'
M. s. purpurascens	Purple Maiden Grass	3–4'
M. s. 'Silberfeder'	Silver Feather	5–7'
M. s. 'Strictus'	Porcupine Grass	6–8'
M. s. 'Variegatus'	Variegated Japanese Silver	5–7'
M. s. 'Zebrinus'	Zebra Grass	5–7'

Natural Landscapes

Latin name	Common name	Height
Andropogon gerardii	Big Blue Stem	4–6'
Bouteloua gracilis	Mosquito Grass	1–2'
Eragrostis trichodes	Sand Love Grass	4–5'
Miscanthus sacchariflorus	Silver Banner Grass	4–6'
Panicum virgatum	Switch Grass	5–6'
Pennisetum flaccidum	Fountain Grass	3–4'
Sporobolus heterolepis	Prairie Dropseed	2–3'

Screening

Latin name	Common name	Height
Calamagrostis × acutiflora 'Stricta'	Feather Reed Grass	5–7'
Erianthus ravennae	Ravenna Grass	9–12'
Miscanthus floridulus	Giant Chinese Silver Grass	8–10'
M. sacchariflorus & cultivars	Silver Banner Grass	4–6'
◆ *Pennisetum alopecuroides*	◆ Fountain Grass	3–4'
Spartina pectinata & cultivars	Prairie Cord Grass	4–6'

NOTES

What to Watch Out For

Plants Subject to Disease

Apple (and all fruit-bearing trees)
Barberry (most varieties)
Cherry
Cotoneaster
Euonymus
Hawthorn
Lilac
Rose varieties
Shadblow

Plants That Need Heavy Pruning

Blue Mist
Butterfly Bush
Deutzia
Hydrangea
Kerria
Mock Orange
Rose varieties
Spirea
Tamarisk
Vitex

Plants Subject to Winterkill

Abelia
Beauty Bush
Butterfly Bush
Boxwood
Hypericum
Kerria
Vitex

Trees That Should Not Be Moved in the Fall

Red or Swamp Maple
Birch varieties
Hornbeam
Dogwood varieties
Hawthorn varieties
Silverbell
Golden Rain Tree
Sweetgum
Tulip Tree

Sycamore
Cherry (and all stone fruit trees)
Pear
Oak
Willow
Styrax
Linden (*tomentosa*)
Zelkova varieties

Shrubs That Thrive on Neglect

Five-leaf Aralia
Azalea
Barberry
Chokeberry
Forsythia
Honeysuckle
Hypericum

Inkberry
Mountain Laurel
Privet
Rhododendron
Viburnum
Winterberry
Witch Hazel

NOTES

Information,
Advice and Inspiration

Societies

The Horticultural Alliance of the Hamptons
Post Office Box 202
Bridgehampton, NY 11932
Tel: 516 537 2223

> Members receive a newsletter with information on local horticultural events. Other benefits include lectures, visits to to public and private gardens and access to the Horticultural Library of the Hamptons.

The American Horticultural Society
Post Office Box 0105
Mount Vernon, VA 22121
Tel: 703 768 5700

> An extensive tour program is available to members, along with special exhibits, conventions and reduced prices on books. A gardener's information service helps you over the phone with specific problems.

The Garden Conservancy
Box 219, Main Street
Cold Spring, NY 10516
Tel: 914 265 2029

> An organization devoted to preserving and maintaining for the public America's most beautiful gardens. Membership benefits include meetings and symposiums, visits to private gardens and a newsletter. Artist Robert Dash's famous garden in Sagaponack is in the Conservancy's trust.

Agencies

United States Department of Agriculture
Soil Conservation Service
Riverhead County Center, Room E16
300 Center Drive
Riverhead, NY 11901-3398
Tel: 516 727 2315

> Technical information and advice on soil conservation and erosion control is provided by telephone. Publications on specific topics are also available.

New York State Department of Environmental Conservation
Building 40
State University of New York
Stony Brook, NY 11790
Tel: 516 751 7900

> The regulating agency responsible for the management and protection of the state's water, land and air resources, and of its marine and wild life.

Dr. Richard Mitchell
New York State Botanist
c/o New York State Museum
Albany, NY 12230
Tel: 518 474 5877

> Information and assistance on rare native plants is provided by phone. Publications and bulletins on specific plants are also available, for a fee.

New York State Office of Parks, Long Island Region
Belmont Lake State Park
Box 247
Babylon, NY 11702
Tel: 516 669 1000, ext. 247

> Owns the Planting Fields Arboretum, PO Box 58, Oyster Bay, NY 11771 (Tel: 516 922 9200) as well as the Bayard Cutting Arboretum, PO Box 466, Oakdale, NY 11769 (Tel: 516 581 1002), both of which are open to the public for ideas and inspiration. Special events are sponsored throughout the year; write or call for schedules.

Suffolk County Cornell Cooperative Extension
246 Griffing Avenue
Riverhead, NY 11901
Tel: 516 727 7850
Horticulture Dept: 516 727 4126

> Provides a wealth of advice on plant diseases and insects, as well as information on conservation of native plants and soil testing. Publications are often available at local libraries.

Planning Departments

East Hampton

All located at:
300 Pantigo Place
East Hampton, NY 11937
>   **Planning Board:** Tel: 516 324 2696
>   **Building Dept:** Tel: 516 324 4145
>   **Natural Resources:** Tel: 516 324 0496

Southampton

All located at:
116 Hampton Road
Southampton, NY 11968
>   **Planning Board, Building Dept, and Natural Resources:** Tel: 516 287 5735

Good Reference Books, Magazines and Catalogs

Books—General

The American Horticultural Society Encyclopedia of Garden Plants
>   Edited by Christopher Brickell, with John Elsley. Macmillan. A comprehensive,
>   illustrated guide to more than 8,000 plants, including 4,000 color photos.

A Dictionary of Plant Names
>   Allen J. Coombes. Timber Press. English in origin, this handy guide gives the
>   pronunciation, botanical and common name equivalents.

Long Island Plants for Landscaping: A Source Book
>   Karen Blumer. Growing Wild Publications. Describes 134 indigenous plants and
>   where they can be purchased, as well as programs, workshops and landscape
>   professionals who specialize in native plants.

The Organic Gardener's Handbook of Natural Insect and Disease Control
>   Edited by Barbara W. Ellis and Fern Marshall Bradley. Rodale Press. Control for
>   a wide range of common insect and disease pests, covering how, when and where
>   to use preventive methods.

Rodale's All New Encyclopedia of Organic Gardening
Edited by Fern Marshall Bradley and Barbara W. Ellis. Rodale Press. For environmentally aware gardeners, this has a terrific section on growing healthy, pesticide-free vegetables and herbs, but covers flowers, trees, shrubs and lawns, too.

Wyman's Gardening Encyclopedia, Updated Edition
Donald Wyman. Macmillan. The author was the horticulturist at the Arnold Arboretum in Boston, and his lifelong love of trees, shrubs and plants is reflected in this easy to use manual.

Books—Trees and Shrubs

Hillier's Manual of Trees and Shrubs, 6th Edition. Trafalgar Square.
From the world-famous Hillier Arboretum, a comprehensive description of 700 trees, shrubs, climbers, conifers and bamboos.

Ornamental Shrubs, Climbers & Bamboos
Graham Stuart Thomas. Sagapress. An easy to use guide to thousands of species, their hybrids and cultivars, described in alphabetical order, with an emphasis on the garden use of shrubs.

Books—Flowers and Grasses

Ornamental Grass Gardening: Design Ideas, Functions and Effects
Thomas A. Reinhardt. Martina Reinhardt & Mark Moskowitz HP Books. Explores the many uses of grasses and shows how they can extend the seasonal duration of your garden. Includes descriptions of the most commonly available grass types.

Perennial Garden Plants; or, The Modern Florilegium, 3rd Edition
Graham Stuart Thomas. Sagapress/Timber Press. Surveys 2,000 species with descriptions that include size, color, spacing, flowering season, propagation and cultivation information.

Roses: An Illustrated Encyclopedia and Grower's Handbook of Species Roses, Old Roses & Modern Roses, Shrub Sroses & Climbers
Peter Beales. Henry Holt. A comprehensive and beautifully illustrated dictionary that covers nearly 2,000 old, modern and species roses.

The Graham Stuart Thomas Rose Book
Graham Stuart Thomas. Sagapress/Timber Press. A compilation of the world-renowned plantsman's three original classics on the subject—*Old Shrub Roses, Climbing Roses Old and New,* and *Shrub Roses of Today*—revised and updated with new color illustrations.

Magazines and Journals

Fine Gardening
> 63 South Main Street, Box 5506
> Newtown, CT 06470
> Tel: 203 426 8171
>
> Beautiful photographs make this news and views magazine appealing. Many subscribers write in to comment or expand on articles from the previous issue.

Horticulture, The Magazine of American Gardening
> 98 North Washington Street
> Boston, MA 02114-1913
> Tel: 617 742 5600
>
> Provides hands on news, views, articles and how-to information for gardeners in the northeastern United States.

Garden Design
> 4401 Connecticut Avenue N.W., Suite 500
> Washington, D.C. 20008-2302
> Tel: 212 686 2752
>
> This beautifully illustrated magazine provides ideas and inspiration for garden designs; as well as sources for garden furniture, ornaments and accessories.

The Journal of the New England Garden History Society
> Massachusetts Horticultural Society
> 300 Massachusetts Avenue
> Boston, MA 02115
> Tel: 617 536 9280
>
> Illustrated, published annually. Fascinating articles and information on the history of gardening, landscape design and the designers of the northeastern region of the United States.

Hortus
> Bryan's Ground
> Stapleton,
> Herefordshire, LD8 2LP
> UK
>
> Privately published four times a year, this is a journal for all who love gardening and good writing. Contributors include most of the best garden writers in the English-speaking world.

Mail Order Catalogs

Applewood Seed Company
5380 Vivian Street
Arvada, CA 80002
Tel. 303 431 7981

Wildflower seeds for specific site conditions, including native varieties.

J. L. Hudson, Seedsman
Post Office Box 1058
Redwood City, CA 94064

Rare seeds from all over the world. No phone orders.

Park Seed
Cokesbury Road
Greenwood, SC 29647-0001
Tel. 1 800 845 3369

Large selection of quality seeds and garden supplies

Roses of Yesterday and Today
802 Brown's Valley Road
Watsonville, CA 95076
Tel. 408 724 3537

Old, rare, unusual and selected modern roses from around the world.

Shepherd's Garden Seeds
30 Irene Street
Torrington, CT 06790
Tel. 203 482 3638

European vegetable and herb varieties and special flower seeds. The catalog is a good read, with vegetarian recipes included.

Thompson & Morgan Inc.
Post Office Box 1308
Jackson, NJ 08527-0308
Tel. 201 363 2225

A huge selection of plants of all types, with good descriptions, germination and cultural information.

Timber Press/Sagapress
9999 SW Wilshire, Suite 124
Portland, OR 97225
Tel. 1 800 327 5680

An outstanding selection of books on all aspects of horticulture and landscape design.

Van Bourgondien & Sons, Inc.
Post Office Box A
245 Farmingdale Road
Babylon, NY 11702
Tel. 1 800 622 9997

> A Long Island importer with a broad selection of bulbs, as well as perennials, berries, ornamental shrubs and houseplants.

Wayside Gardens
Post Office Box 1
Hodges, SC 29695
Tel. 1 800 845 1124

> Beautifully illustrated, this catalog accurately describes a wide variety of flowering plants. It's a great tool to use when you are planning a garden. Ornamental trees and shrubs, perennials and roses, with good cultural information provided by Wayside's Culture Cards.

NOTES

ABOUT THE BAYBERRY NURSERY

The Bayberry Nursery site includes a twelve-acre arboretum with over 3,500 rare specimen trees and a retail garden center. It offers a wide range of antique and contemporary garden accessories including teak furniture, copper lanterns, weather vanes, sundials, bird and bat houses, sculpture, bronze and stone ornaments, fountains and handcrafted pottery.

Stonyhill Nursery, the Bayberry's 82-acre tree farm in Amagansett, supplies most of the trees and shrubs (including many native varieties) that are sold at the nursery.

Most of the 60 members of the staff are native Long Islanders, and their average tenure at The Bayberry is eleven years. They include:

Robert Strubel, General Manager garden center
    degree: State University of New York, ornamental horticulture.
Kenneth Pascual, Manager design studio
    degree: University of New Hampshire, plant science, *cum laude*.
Teresa Pascual, Designer ornamental gardens
    degree: State University of New York, agriculture.
    Rutgers University design courses.
Judy Comfort, Manager office and retail store

Located on Montauk Highway, just west of the village of Amagansett, The Bayberry is open seven days a week from March until December. Telephone: (516) 267-3000.

105

About the Author

David Seeler has owned and operated the Bayberry Nursery since 1970. He has a degree in landscape architecture from the University of Georgia, and a degree in ornamental horticulture from the State University of New York. His work has been featured in publications including *The New York Times, House and Garden* and *The Hamptons Magazine*. From 1970 to 1976 he developed the famous Alfonso Ossorio estate "The Creeks" in East Hampton, which has perhaps the finest collection of rare plants in the northeastern United States.

Acknowledgments

My grateful thanks to Ralph Carpentier and Teresa Pascual for the illustrations; Stephanie Clark for her editorial help; Kenneth Pascual for design graphics; and Neal Bastable for landscape architectural drawings. Also my thanks to Gerald and Susan Hobbs and Herman and Ruth Widder for the use of their landscape plans; to Janet Hummel for her excellent typing; to Margaret Kaplan, Pamela Lord, Maria Matthiesson and Robert Strubel for invaluable advice; to Gerry McCallion and Liz Robinson for meticulous proofreading; and to all my customers and friends who have made my career a challenge and a pleasure.

Illustrations

Illustrations by Ralph Carpentier on jacket and pages iv, vi, x, 2–3, 5, 7, 9, 15, and 108–109;
by Teresa Pascual on pages iii, 16, 24, 25, 33, 34, 35, 37, 39, 41, 43, 44, 47, 48, 49, 51, 54, 55, 57, 59, 62, 63, 65, 68–69, 74, 79, 80, 81, 85, 87, and 90–91;
and by Eva Auchincloss on page 105.
Plan on page 11 by Perry Guillot, landscape architect.

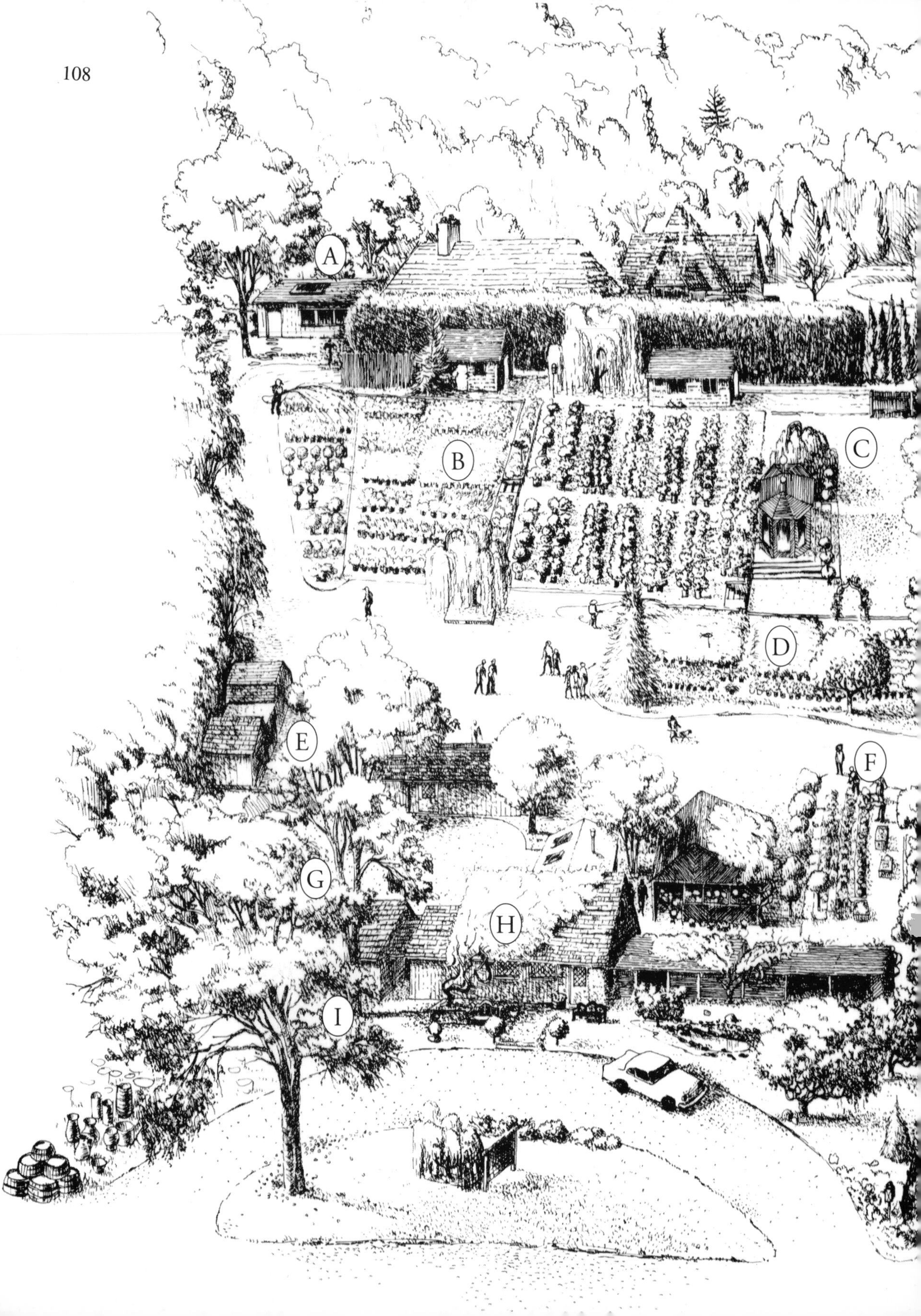
A
B
C
D
E
F
G
H
I

BAYBERRY · DIRECTORY ·

A Design Studio
B Container Plants
C Roses
D Perennials
E Garden Supplies
F Herbs and Gourmet Vegetables
G Administrative Office
H Gifts, Antiques
I Pottery, Garden Ornaments
J 3,500 Dwarf and Rare Plant Collection
K Specimen Trees and Shrubs
L Teak Garden Furniture
M Pond
N Barn
O Ornamental Grass Garden
P Annuals